WELCOME TO MY COUNTRY

Welcome to
COSTA RICA

Gareth Stevens Publishing
A WORLD ALMANAC EDUCATION GROUP COMPANY

Written by
ROSALIE GARRETT/NICOLE FRANK

Edited in USA by
DOROTHY L. GIBBS

Designed by
JAILANI BASARI

Picture research by
SUSAN JANE MANUEL

First published in North America in 2001 by
Gareth Stevens Publishing
A World Almanac Education Group Company
330 West Olive Street, Suite 100
Milwaukee, Wisconsin 53212 USA

Please visit our web site at:
www.garethstevens.com
For a free color catalog describing
Gareth Stevens' list of high-quality books
and multimedia programs, call
1-800-542-2595 (USA) or
1-800-461-9120 (CANADA).
Gareth Stevens Publishing's
Fax: (414) 332-3567.

© **TIMES MEDIA PRIVATE LIMITED 2001**
Originated and designed by
Times Editions
An imprint of Times Media Private Limited
A member of the Times Publishing Group
Times Centre, 1 New Industrial Road
Singapore 536196
http://www.timesone.com.sg/te

Library of Congress Cataloging-in-Publication Data
Garrett, Rosalie.
Welcome to Costa Rica / Rosalie Garrett and Nicole Frank.
p. cm. — (Welcome to my country)
Includes bibliographical references and index.
ISBN 0-8368-2523-3 (lib. bdg.)
1. Costa Rica—Juvenile literature. [1. Costa Rica.]
I. Frank, Nicole. II. Title. III. Series.
FI543.2 .G37   2001
972.8605—dc21   2001017028

Printed in Malaysia

1 2 3 4 5 6 7 8 9 05 04 03 02 01

PICTURE CREDITS
A.N.A. Press Agency: 26, 27
Archive Photos: 5 (bottom), 16, 17, 35, 38
Camera Press: 15 (bottom)
DDB Stock Photo: 15 (top)
Focus Team–Italy: 3 (center), 5 (top),
    19 (bottom), 23, 29, 37
Robert Francis: 19 (top)
Dave G. Houser: 2, 7, 30, 34, 40
The Hutchison Library: 20, 33, 43, 45
Björn Klingwall: 21, 28
Jason Laure: 39
Michael J. Pettypool: 9
Pietro Scozzari: cover
David Simson: 22, 24, 25
South American Pictures: 13, 14, 31
Topham Picturepoint: 1, 3 (top and bottom),
    10, 11, 18
Trip Photographic Library: 6
Vision Photo Agency/Hulton Getty: 12
Nik Wheeler: 4, 8, 32, 36, 41

Digital Scanning by Superskill Graphics Pte Ltd

Contents

Words that appear in the glossary are printed in **boldface** type the first time they occur in the text.

Welcome to Costa Rica!

Costa Rica is one of seven countries in Central America. It is known for its rain forests and its many kinds of plant and animal life. Some people who visit Costa Rica call it Earth's natural park. Let's explore Costa Rica and meet its people!

The Flag of Costa Rica

The current Costa Rican flag was adopted in 1848. It has stripes of blue, white, and red. The blue stripes represent faith and justice. The white stripes stand for **purity**. The red stripe in the center has a white oval that contains the country's national **shield**.

The Land

Costa Rica covers only 19,730 square miles (51,101 square kilometers). It is one of the smallest countries in Central America. Nicaragua is north of Costa Rica. Panama is to the south. The Caribbean Sea is along the eastern coastline, and the Pacific Ocean is along the western coastline. The capital of Costa Rica is San José.

Below: Tortuga Island is a private nature reserve. It is located south of the Nicoya Peninsula, in the Pacific Ocean.

Costa Rica has three geographical areas — the Pacific coast, the central highlands, and the Caribbean lowlands. The Pacific coast has steep cliffs and sandy beaches. The central highlands, called the Meseta Central, have valleys of rich soil bordered by mountain ranges. This area is ideal for growing coffee, one of Costa Rica's most important crops. The Caribbean lowlands are flat plains along the eastern coastline.

Above: Póas Volcano is one of the deepest active volcanoes in the world. It is 8,885 feet (2,708 meters) high. One of its craters contains a rain-fed lake.

Climate

Costa Rica has a **tropical** climate. The average temperature along the coast is 84° Fahrenheit (29° Celsius). The average temperature in the highlands is 72° F (22° C). Rainfall determines the country's two seasons. The dry season lasts from December through May. The rainy season lasts from June through November.

Above: Because Costa Rica is close to the **equator**, trees and other plants bloom all year long.

Plants and Animals

Costa Rica is famous for its rain forests. Thousands of plant species, including over 2,000 types of trees and 1,200 kinds of orchids, grow throughout the country. Unfortunately, **deforestation** is a continuing problem.

Costa Rica also has a wide variety of animals, including jaguars, turtles, anteaters, and 162 species of snakes.

Below: The three-toed sloth is one of many unusual animals that live in Costa Rica.

9

History

Before the Spanish came to Costa Rica in the sixteenth century, only groups of native Indians lived there. These groups often fought each other for control of the land.

Christopher Columbus was the first European to set foot on Costa Rican soil. He landed on September 18, 1502. When the Spaniards tried to bring the

Left: Because the native Indians of Costa Rica greeted him with gifts of gold, Christopher Columbus called the land "Rich Coast of Veragua."

native peoples under their control, the Indian groups joined forces and fought fiercely to keep their freedom. By the 1560s, many Indians had died either of diseases or by fighting. Most of the Indians who survived became Christians. As Christians, they were allowed to live in Spanish settlements and **intermarry** with the Europeans.

Above: Columbus did not find gold in Costa Rica. In fact, Costa Rica turned out to be one of Spain's poorest colonies.

Independence

In 1821, after the Spanish Empire had been weakened by wars with Britain and France, Mexico and the Central American provinces, which included Costa Rica, declared their independence. At first, Costa Rica became part of the Mexican Empire. In 1823, however, it joined four other Central American states to form the United Provinces of Central America. Costa Rica became a completely independent country in 1838.

Becoming a Democracy

In 1856, William Walker, who named himself president of Nicaragua in 1855, tried to invade Costa Rica. Costa Rican forces, led by Juan Rafael Mora Porras, defeated Walker. Mora Porras held power until 1870, when General Tomás Guardia Gitiérrez **seized** the presidency.

Left: William Walker (1824–1860) was an American adventurer, born in Tennessee. Although his attempt to invade Costa Rica was unsuccessful, he controlled Nicaragua for two years.

In 1890, Costa Rica held the first free elections in Central American history and became the region's first **democracy**. Rafael Angel Calderón Guardia, who was president from 1940 to 1944, passed important laws that guaranteed basic rights to Costa Rican citizens. He also developed a social security system for the country.

War and Peace

Calderón ran for president again in 1948 but lost to Otilio Ulate Blanco. When Calderón refused to accept Ulate's election, a **civil war** began. A landowner named José Figueres Ferrer formed the National Liberation Party (PLN), which fought for Ulate's government. At the end of the war, Figueres himself took power.

Since then, Costa Rica has enjoyed peace, even through the 1980s and 1990s, when other Central American countries were having civil wars and political conflicts.

Juan Santamaría (c. 1839–1856)

Although only about seventeen when he died, Juan Santamaría became Costa Rica's first national hero. During the war against William Walker, Santamaría set fire to the enemy's buildings. He died during the battle.

Juan Santamaría

Sonia Picado Sotela (1936–)

Now a member of Costa Rica's Congress, Sonia Picado Sotela has held powerful political positions. In 1996, she became the Costa Rican **ambassador** to the United States.

Oscar Arias Sánchez (1949–)

As president of Costa Rica from 1986 to 1990, Oscar Arias Sánchez played a key role in bringing peace to Central America. He won the Nobel Prize for Peace in 1987.

Oscar Arias Sánchez

Government and the Economy

Costa Rica is a **democratic republic**. Its government has three branches — legislative, executive, and judicial.

The legislative branch is called the Legislative Assembly. Its fifty-seven members are Costa Rica's lawmakers. The president, two vice presidents, and a Council of Government form the executive

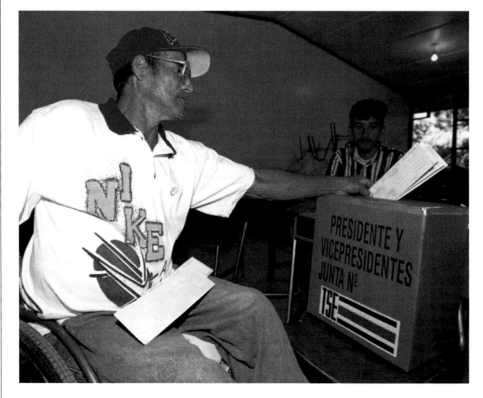

Left: Presidential elections are held every four years in Costa Rica. A candidate must receive at least 40 percent of the vote to become the country's president.

branch. The Council of Government has eighteen ministers who enforce national laws and establish foreign policies. The Supreme Court leads the judicial branch.

The two major political parties in Costa Rica are the PLN and the Social Christian Unity Party (PUSC). Most members of the Legislative Assembly belong to one of these two parties.

Economy

The Costa Rican economy depends mainly on tourism, agriculture, and raising cattle. Tourism is one of the most important sources of **revenue**. About 700,000 people visit Costa Rica every year. The banana industry is very important, too. Bananas make up one-fifth of the country's **exports**.

Left: The large areas of grassland in the province of Guanacaste are ideal for raising cattle. Beef is Costa Rica's third largest export.

Costa Rica also exports pineapples, coffee, beef, plastics, and electronics. Among the country's main **imports** are raw materials for industry, fuels, transportation, and construction.

More than a million people are employed in Costa Rica. Most of them have service jobs, such as working in hotels and hospitals or selling real estate. Twenty-two percent work in agriculture, and 17 percent work in industry.

People and Lifestyle

Most Costa Ricans are either white or *mestizo* (mays-TEE-soh), which are people of mixed Spanish and native Indian ancestry. Costa Rica also has a few minority groups.

Afro-Costa Ricans are the largest minority group. They have Jamaican roots and live along the Caribbean coast. Afro-Costa Ricans speak English instead of Spanish. The native Indians

Below: Many people gather at the Plaza de la Cultura in San José, where they can visit museums, shops, and cafés.

Above: Most
native Indians in
Costa Rica live
in communities
near the southern
border and make
a living by farming.

that lived in Costa Rica before the
Spanish arrived now make up less
than 3 percent of the population.
Other minority groups are Chinese,
Italians, and Germans.

Over two-thirds of the population
live in the Meseta Central, where San
José, the country's capital, is located.
Although Costa Rica has both rich
and poor people, most Costa Ricans
are middle-class and well-educated.

Family Life

Family is very important to all Costa Ricans, but Costa Rican women traditionally have been expected to take more responsibility for their families than men.

Costa Rican Society

The roles of men and women in Costa Rican society are defined by the terms *machismo* (mah-CHEES-moh) and

Below: "Queen Bee" families are common in some areas of Costa Rica. In these families, a woman is head of the household and works to earn a living.

marianismo (mah-ree-ahn-EES-moh). Machismo is the idea that men are more important than women. Men are expected to be strong and proud. They receive more privileges in society than women, and they rarely help with housework.

Marianismo is the idea that women should be **self-sacrificing**. Women are expected to respect their husbands and do all the household chores.

Above: From a young age, Costa Rican boys are taught to be brave, **aggressive**, and strong. They are expected to do manly activities, such as repair cars and play sports.

Education

Costa Rica has the highest literacy rate in Central America. Approximately 95 percent of its people can read and write. Education has been free in Costa Rica since 1886.

The country has four schools of higher learning that are supported by the government. The oldest, the University of Costa Rica in San José, opened in 1940. Costa Rica is also

Above: Children in Costa Rica must attend school until the age of fourteen.

home to the University for Peace, which is a school sponsored by the United Nations.

Although the education system in Costa Rica is the best in Central America, it still has its problems. Classrooms are overcrowded, and teachers are often poorly paid and not well-trained. Many Costa Ricans think the **curriculum** needs to be updated to offer students more practical experience.

Below:
These students are enjoying a break between classes at a Costa Rican university.

Religion

Costa Rica's 1949 constitution made Roman Catholicism the country's national religion. Costa Ricans are free to practice any Christian religion, but more than 90 percent of them are Roman Catholics.

Holy Week, or *Semana Santa* (say-MAHN-ah SAHN-tah), is a national holiday in Costa Rica. It takes place every spring, with

Below: When they get married, most Costa Ricans have a church ceremony. Then they join family and friends for a celebration with food, music, and dancing.

thousands of people participating in celebrations and processions held throughout the week.

The Virgin Mary and other Catholic saints are very important in Costa Rica. People pray to their favorite saints for help. On August 2, thousands of Costa Ricans travel to Cartago to pray to the *Virgen de los Angeles* (VAIR-hen day lohs AHN-hail-ays).

Above: The Cartago Basilica holds the statue of the Virgen de los Angeles, who has been the patron saint of Costa Rica since 1782.

Language

Most people in Costa Rica speak Spanish. It is the country's official language. Due to a large number of English-speaking immigrants and tourists, many Costa Ricans can also speak and understand English.

The Spanish spoken in Costa Rica is slightly different from the Spanish spoken in Spain. For example, in Spain, *tú* means "you," when speaking to friends. In Costa Rica, *tú* does not exist. *Usted* or *vos* is used instead.

Below: With a growing number of English-speaking tourists visiting Costa Rica, signs for many popular attractions have information in both Spanish and English.

Literature

Most Costa Rican novels and short stories feature *costumbrismo* (koh-stoom-BREES-moh), or local color. Their authors write about the lives of peasants and farmers in local settings.

Carlos Luis Fallas is one of Costa Rica's most **influential** literary figures. His book, *Mamita Yunai,* describes the terrible living and working conditions on banana plantations. Although written in 1941, *Mamita Yunai* is still required reading in Costa Rican schools.

Arts

Costa Rica has many artists, especially in San José. The forms of art in Costa Rica include making jewelry, pottery, and wood carvings.

Oxcarts

Carretas (kah-RAY-tahs), or colorful oxcarts, are a national symbol of Costa Rica. Painting oxcarts started nearly

Below: Oxcarts of all sizes are still made and painted today in Sarchí, the crafts capital of Costa Rica. Miniature oxcarts are very popular souvenirs, and tourists sometimes even paint these carts themselves.

one hundred years ago. At that time, oxcarts were used to **transport** coffee beans from the fields to the coasts. Local artists painted designs on the oxcarts to identify the regions to which they belonged.

Each year, the town of San Antonio de Escazú has a festival with oxcart parades. It is called *Día de los Boyeros* (DEE-ah day lohs boy-AIR-ohs), which means Day of the Oxcart Drivers.

Above: At the Día de los Boyeros festival, hundreds of cowboys and their families ride around the town of San Antonio de Escazú in decorated oxcarts.

Nicoya Pottery

The small town of Guaitíl is famous for Nicoya pottery. This pottery was first made in the northwestern part of Costa Rica around A.D. 500. It is known for its colorful designs and special molding technique. The clay is rolled into **coils** before it is shaped and decorated. Designs are painted on in red, black, yellow, and cream colors.

Below: Recently, the women of Guaitíl started making Nicoya pottery again. This art had not been practiced for centuries.

Music and Dancing

Costa Ricans love music and dancing. San José is the home of Costa Rica's National Symphony Orchestra. Talented musicians, conductors, and singers from all over the world perform classical music with this orchestra.

The *punto guanacasteco* (POON-toh gwon-ah-kass-TAY-koh) is Costa Rica's national dance. It is a folk dance that involves a lot of stomping.

Above: Dancers often wear colorful costumes when they perform traditional Costa Rican folk dances.

Leisure

Costa Ricans enjoy their free time. Some like to play sports, others attend cultural events. In the cities, people like to eat at restaurants and go to movies. Every March, arts festivals offer music, dancing, and theater from all over the world. On weekends, Costa Ricans will often visit one of their country's thirty-five national parks.

Left: Because eating out is not very expensive, it is a good way for Costa Ricans to enjoy time with family and friends.

The National Theater

Going to the theater is an extremely popular activity in Costa Rica. Some people think this country has more theater companies than any other country in the world. Since 1897, hundreds of people, including the National Symphony Orchestra, have performed at the National Theater in San José. This **lavish** building is Costa Rica's cultural center.

Sports

Because they have beautiful, warm weather all year round, Costa Ricans are able to play and watch many outdoor sports, from baseball to bullfighting. Soccer, however, is, by far, the country's most popular sport. Costa Rica's champion soccer team is from San José. The team is called Saprissa, but it is also known as *El Monstro*, which means "The Monster."

Below: Every town and village in Costa Rica, no matter how small, has at least one soccer team.

Baseball is popular in Costa Rica, too, especially in the city of Limón. Other favorite outdoor sports in Costa Rica are tennis and bicycle racing.

Costa Rica's oceans and rivers are ideal for water sports, such as scuba diving, surfing, fishing, and snorkeling. Lake Arenal in northern Costa Rica is well-known by windsurfers around the world. The constant gusty winds in this area provide perfect windsurfing conditions all year long.

Above: White-water rafting is becoming a popular sport in Costa Rica. The country has rivers and rapids for every level of rafting skill, from beginner to expert.

Festivals

In Costa Rica, most of the festivals are religious. Every town has a celebration each year to honor its own patron saint. A national holiday on August 2 honors the country's patron saint, the Virgen de los Angeles.

Christmas is a special time in Costa Rica. The celebration begins in late November and, for many Costa Ricans, lasts until New Year's Day.

Left: Each year, thousands of Costa Ricans gather along the streets of Cartago to watch the procession of the Virgen de los Angeles.

For nine days each July, the town of Alajuela holds a Mango Festival. This celebration includes arts and crafts fairs, parades, food, and music.

September 15 is Costa Rica's Independence Day. On this day in 1821, Costa Rica and the rest of Central America became independent from Spain. Colorful parades highlight the Independence Day celebrations, and the Costa Rican flag flies proudly throughout the country.

Above: Costa Rica celebrates Children's Day on September 9. Instead of going to school on this day, children take part in parades, dances, and other exciting events and activities.

Food

In the Costa Rican diet, rice, beans, and maize, or corn, are part of almost every meal, from breakfast to dinner. The breakfast dish called *gallo pinto* (GUY-yoh PEEN-toh), or "spotted rooster," contains black beans, rice, onions, and spices. *Casado* (cah-SAH-doh), a popular lunchtime dish, is rice served with beans, eggs, meat, and vegetables.

Left: Costa Ricans can buy fresh fruits and vegetables at the central market in San José.

Many restaurants and cafés in Costa Rica serve small snacks called *bocas* (BOH-cahs). Bocas can be potato chips, tortillas with cheese, chicken wings, fish cooked in spices and juices, or even turtle eggs.

Beverages

Coffee is a popular drink in Costa Rica. Another favorite is sugar water, called *agua dulce* (AH-gwah DOOL-say).

COSTA RICA

Country Border
Capital
City
River

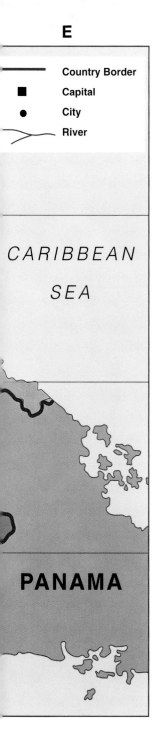

CARIBBEAN

SEA

PANAMA

Above: Cabo Blanco Strict Nature Reserve on the Nicoya Peninsula is the oldest protected area in Costa Rica.

Gulf of Dulce D4
Gulf of Nicoya
   B2–B3

Heredia (city) C2
Heredia (province)
   C1–C2

Lake Arenal B1
Limón (city) D2
Limón (province)
   D1–D3

Meseta Central C2

Nicaragua B1–C1
Nicoya A2
Nicoya Peninsula
   A2–B2

Osa Peninsula D4

Pacific Ocean
   A1–E4

Panama E3–E4
Poás Volcano C2
Puntarenas
   (province) B2–D4

Reventazón River
   C2–D2
Río Grande de
   Tárcoles B2–C2
Río Grande de
   Térraba D3
Rivas A1

San Antonio de
   Escazú C2
San Carlos River
   B1–C1
San José (city) C2
San José (province)
   C2–D3
Sarapiquí River
   C1–C2
Sarchí C2

Tortuga Island B3

Cordillera de
   Talamanca D3

Frio River B1

Guaitíl A2
Guanacaste
   (province) A1–B2

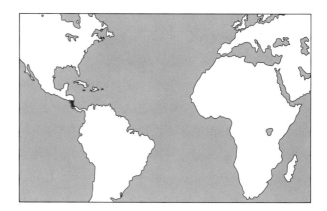

Quick Facts

Official Name   Republic of Costa Rica

Capital   San José

Official Language   Spanish

Population   3,710,558 (2000 estimate)

Land Area   19,730 square miles (51,101 square km)

Provinces   Alajuela, Cartago, Guanacaste, Heredia, Limón, Puntarenas, San José

Major Cities   Alajuela, Cartago, Heredia, San José

Highest Point   Cerro Chirripó 12,530 feet (3,819 m)

Major Mountains   Cordillera de Talamanca

Major Rivers   Frio River, Reventazón River, Río Grande de Tárcoles, Río Grande de Térraba

Main Religion   Roman Catholicism

Important Holidays   Semana Santa (April)

La Virgen de los Angeles (August 2)

Independence Day (September 15)

Christmas (December)

Currency   Colón (315.91 colóns = U.S. $1 in 2001)

Opposite: The Church of La Merced is located in the center of San José.

Glossary

aggressive: forceful and bold, sometimes in an unfriendly way.

ambassador: an official representative sent by one country to live in another to help the governments of those countries work together.

civil war: a war between sections of the same country or different groups of citizens within that country.

coils: material wound around and around in circles or spirals.

curriculum: the kinds of coursework a school offers.

deforestation: the destruction of forests by cutting down or burning trees to clear the land.

democracy: a system of government by the people in which citizens freely elect their own representatives.

democratic republic: a country, or nation, with a democratic form of government.

equator: the imaginary line around the middle of Earth, which is the area that stays closest to the Sun as Earth rotates.

exports: goods sent out of a country to sell to other countries.

imports: goods brought into a country, which have been purchased from other countries.

influential: having a powerful affect on the thoughts or actions of others.

intermarry: get married to a person who belongs to a different religious, cultural, or ethnic group.

landmark: a recognizable building, place, or landform that serves as a guide to a particular location.

lavish: richly and heavily decorated.

purity: a clean or innocent condition, untouched by anything dirty, evil, or unhealthy.

revenue: money that comes from sales or taxes and is used to support a government or organization.

seized: took by force.

self-sacrificing: giving up personal needs and interests so others can have what they need or want.

shield: a badge or coat of arms used as the official symbol of a group.

transport: carry or move from one place to another.

tropical: hot and humid.

More Books to Read

Costa Rica. Enchantment of the World series. Marion Morrison (Children's Press)

Costa Rica. Festivals of the World series. Frederick Fisher (Gareth Stevens)

Costa Rica. Globe-Trotters Club series. Tracey West (Carolrhoda Books)

Costa Rica in Pictures. Visual Geography series. Sandra Sawicki (Lerner)

Fernando's Gift. Douglas Keister (Little, Brown & Co.)

The Forest in the Clouds. Sneed B. Collard III (Charlesbridge)

Jungle Jumble. Mark Wainwright (Mark Wainwright)

When Woman Became the Sea: A Costa Rican Creation Myth. Susan Strauss (Beyond Words)

Videos

The Birds and Wildlife of Costa Rica. (Superior Home Video)

Costa Rica & Belize. (IVN Entertainment)

The Wonders of the Deep: Costa Rica/ Cocos Island/The Galapagos. (Madacy Entertainment)

Web Sites

www.calnative.com/n_oxcart.htm

www.geocities.com/The Tropics/3425

www.sio.ucsd.edu/volcano

www.tourism-costarica.com

Due to the dynamic nature of the Internet, some web sites stay current longer than others. To find additional web sites, use a reliable search engine with one or more of the following keywords to help you locate information about Costa Rica. Keywords: *bananas, Guaitíl, Nicoya peninsula, Juan Santamaría, Tortuga Island.*

Index